Everyone was talking about him. It didn't matter where you went. In the towns, in the villages, in the market or down by the water's edge, everyone was talking about him: Jesus of Nazareth.

Andrew and I talked about Jesus when we went fishing in our boat. And we talked about him with our friends and business partners, James and John, as we sat by the edge of Lake Galilee, sorting our fish or mending our nets. It didn't matter what we were talking about – the weather, the Romans, or local gossip. No matter what the topic of conversation, we always ended up talking about Jesus. He was different. And he was interesting. Really, really interesting.

It was just an ordinary day, much like any other. We'd been out fishing all night and we hadn't caught a single fish. Not one!

Not even a tiddler. I was exhausted, shattered with lack of sleep. I just wanted to go home, have a rest and something to eat before having another go at earning a living.

"We'd better sort the nets out first," said Andrew.

I grunted. Sorting the nets was the last thing I wanted to do, but I knew he was right. It had to be done.

I helped James and John drag the boats to the shore, and then the four of us carried the empty nets to the shore, ready to be washed.

I heard a noise and looked up. I could see a crowd of people making their way down the hillside, the colours of their cloaks and tunics shining in the early morning sunshine.

At the head of the crowd walked a man. I knew who it was straight away. No one else had crowds following him like that. It was Jesus! Jesus of Nazareth!

"Let me tell you what God's kingdom is like," Jesus' voice boomed across the water, "and how he wants you to live..."

The crowd pressed forwards, following

Jesus every step of the way, keen to catch everything he said.

"If they don't give him some space they'll never hear a thing," I muttered under my breath, scrubbing at the net between my clenched fists.

I felt a hand on my shoulder and I looked up. Jesus was standing right behind me. I stood up straight and looked at the faces of the crowd, staring back at me.

"Simon Peter," said Jesus. He was smiling at me.

"Yes Jesus," I said. I couldn't help smiling back at him. Whenever I was with him nothing else mattered. Not even washing out the nets.

"Simon Peter," said Jesus. "I think I need to borrow your boat for a while. Take me a little way from the shore, and I'll talk to the people from your boat – if you don't mind...?"

Mind? Of course I didn't mind. I leapt up, helped Jesus aboard, tucked my tunic in my belt and pushed the boat out across the lake, before clambering in and anchoring the boat to face the crowds.

"Now," said Jesus. His voice boomed towards the land, and the crowd settled contentedly on the ground, ready to listen. "Where was I? Oh, yes. Let me tell you what God's kingdom is like..."

I sat in the boat and listened along with the rest, spellbound by everything I heard, while the boat gently rocked to the lapping water of the lake.

After a while Jesus stopped talking and the people began to make their way up the hillside, back to their homes.

"Now Simon Peter," said Jesus looking at me.

"Yes?" I said and yawned. I couldn't help it. I had been up all night.

"Sail to the middle of the lake," said Jesus. "When you are there, put your nets in the water, ready to catch some fish!"

I groaned. All I wanted to do was go home. And I still hadn't finished washing my nets.

"I've been fishing all night," I said, sighing deeply. "And I didn't catch a thing. There's no point going out again."

I looked at Jesus and pulled a face. But he didn't say anything. He just kept looking at me.

"All right!" I said, putting my hands up in a gesture of surrender. "You win! I'll go to the middle of the lake and put down my nets. But I'm only doing it because you asked me to."

Jesus nodded and smiled. Then he got out of the boat and watched me from the shore as I sailed out across the lake.

James and John looked up from the shore. So did Andrew. "Where are you going?"

he yelled.

"Fishing!" I yelled back.

"Wait for me!" he shouted and swam towards the boat.

We sailed out in silence, towards the deepest water of the lake, and then we lifted the nets and flung them into the water.

I turned round to face the shore, and saw Jesus waiting, watching.

Suddenly the boat lurched sideways and the ropes of the nets creaked and groaned.

"Fish!" yelled Andrew, hanging over the side of the boat trying to tug the nets in. "The nets are full of fish! Help me Peter!"

I stumbled towards Andrew, grabbed the net and heaved as hard as I could, digging my heels into the side of the boat!

"Help!" we shouted to James and John, hardly daring to let go of the nets to wave to them. "Come and help us!" I called.

As soon as James and John drew their boat alongside, we heaved together, dragging the nets aboard each of the boats, watching hundreds of fish as they slithered and squirmed their way across the floor.

I felt the boat drop in the water. It was so

heavy! I glanced across at James. He looked shocked. "Any more fish and we'll sink!" he said.

I nodded and we slowly made our way towards the shore and the waiting figure of Jesus.

As soon as I climbed out of the boat I ran to Jesus. "Jesus... master... I... I..." I couldn't get my words out. There was so much I wanted to say. I had never seen anything like it! It was a miracle! I knelt at his feet and looked up at him. He looked so ordinary, just like one of us. And yet I knew he wasn't ordinary at all.

"Who are you?" I whispered looking at him. "You are so amazing! What are you doing spending your time with someone like me?"

"Don't be afraid," said Jesus. "Come and be with me. Follow me. Learn to catch men and women for God!"

Suddenly that was the only thing I wanted to do. I was done with fishing! I wanted to be with Jesus. I dragged my boat onto the shore and followed him.

Chapter Two

I tell you, after that, my life wasn't the same. I did the odd spot of fishing, but most of the time I followed Jesus, into the towns, into the villages, up in the hills and along by the lakeside.

James and John came too. So did Andrew. As soon as Jesus asked us to follow him we all did the same thing. We left our boats and became Jesus' followers: his disciples. Eventually there were twelve of us who were Jesus' special friends, but there were loads of people who were his followers.

But life didn't change just for us. It changed for so many people. Everyone who met Jesus was affected by him in some small way.

One day we were out in one of the towns when a man came up to Jesus. He was covered in sores and little white spots. I knew at once it was leprosy. He looked revolting.

He shouldn't be allowed out, I thought to myself. Anyone could catch what he's got.

I wrapped my cloak over my mouth and shuffled back, trying to keep out of the way.

I watched as the man fell down at Jesus' feet, and I felt my mouth turn down in disgust.

"Jesus!" said the man, his face to the ground. "I know that if you want, you can make me better!"

Huh! I thought. Impossible! Not even Jesus could do a thing like that.

But to my amazement, Jesus bent down and touched the man. He actually touched him! I looked at his face, and I could see that Jesus really liked him, loved him even. He was smiling at him.

"And I want to make you better!" said Jesus, and he lifted the man's pitted and scarred face in his hands. "So – get better!"

I blinked. And then I blinked again! For in that moment the man's face had changed. So had his fingers and hands. His leprosy had gone! He was completely well.

"Wow!" I gasped. "Wow! Did you see that? Did you see...?"

I looked at my friends – and I could tell that they had seen exactly what I had.

"A miracle!" whistled John. "There's no other word to describe it. That's a miracle!"

But there were so many miracles! Every day something amazing happened. On one occasion Jesus was teaching in somebody's house. It was absolutely packed. There was no room whatsoever. There were people at the windows and there was a crowd waiting outside, hoping to hear or see something – anything.

Suddenly, I heard a scraping sound, and a whole load of mud and straw dropped into my lap. I looked up and I could see four faces poking through the roof!

Really, I said to myself. The things people will do to get a glimpse of Jesus.

I sat there with my mouth open, wondering what was going to happen next, when the four faces disappeared, and a man on a mattress was lowered through the hole, right to where Jesus was standing!

Everyone was speechless. We just sat there, watching.

As soon as I saw the man I knew he couldn't move. He was paralysed.

Jesus looked up, and four faces looked down at him. He nodded at them and smiled, as if he knew exactly what they were thinking. Then Jesus looked at the man on the mattress.

"You have been forgiven for all the wrong things you have done," said Jesus.

"How dare he say that!" someone whispered angrily. I glanced towards the direction of the voice. It was a Pharisee. Lots of them had turned up to hear what Jesus had to say. "Only God can say that. Who does he think he is?"

Jesus spoke and his voice silenced the whispering. "Why are you saying these things?" he asked, staring at the Pharisees, as if he knew who the whisperers were. Then he swung round and faced the paralysed man.

"Get up and walk!" he said. It was like a command. It was as if Jesus had real power and authority. Everything in the room went completely silent and still, and a strange feeling came over me, like the moment before a storm. "Pick up your mattress and go home!"

Suddenly the man leapt to his feet. He bent down and picked up his mattress! "Praise God!" he shouted. "Praise God!"

"Praise God!" murmured everyone in the room. "Praise God!" I repeated over and over again.

I knew that the man's life would never be

the same again. He could walk, and run and move! But no one who had seen what had happened would ever be the same again either.

And for that matter, neither would I!

Chapter Three

Everywhere we went, people were queuing up to see Jesus. If they were ill, they wanted him to touch them, to make them better. If they weren't ill, they wanted to see what was going to happen or to hear some of the things he said.

Jesus was really easy to listen to. He wasn't boring, like some of the Pharisees in the synagogue, who went on and on and on about things all the time. Jesus told stories about ordinary things, which everyone could understand. But as you listened to the stories you realised that Jesus wasn't *just* telling you a story about everyday things, he was talking about something bigger, much much bigger.

Of course some people wanted to catch Jesus out, make him say something wrong that would get him into trouble.

Once, this person who thought he was a

real expert asked Jesus what he had to do to live with God for ever!

Honestly! Even I could have answered that one. Anyone could who's a Jew like me, and had been taught the Scriptures. The answer's simple. You have to love God with all your heart and you have to love your neighbour like you love yourself. Simple! Only it's not so simple, is it?

"Well," said the expert. "Who is my neighbour?"

I could have answered that one too! I thought. Even a simple fisherman knows your neighbour is the person who lives next door!

But before I had a chance to open my mouth, Jesus began to speak.

"One day," said Jesus, "a man was walking from Jerusalem to Jericho."

"Dangerous road," said the man next to me and shook his head. I nodded in agreement. It certainly was.

"A gang of thieves was lying in wait," continued Jesus. "They pounced on the man, ripped his clothes, stole everything he had and left him for dead."

"It can happen," said the man next to me.

"A priest walked down the road," said Jesus, "but when he saw the man, he didn't stop. Instead, he quickly crossed over and walked by on the other side of the road."

I shook my head and wondered what would happen next.

"After that a Levite came along," said Jesus.

"He'll do the right thing," I whispered. "After all, he is supposed to be very good and know all about God."

"So was the priest," shrugged the man next to me.

"Shh," said a voice from behind.

"He stopped and looked at the injured man," continued Jesus, "but then he crossed over the road."

I was surprised that he had turned away as well.

"Along came a Samaritan," said Jesus.

Well he won't help, I thought. Everyone knows Samaritans are no good.

"When the Samaritan saw the injured man he felt sorry for him," said Jesus.

Then, don't tell me, I thought. I know what happens next. He crosses over the road and goes on with his journey.

"The Samaritan cleaned the injured man's wounds and bandaged them up."

"Wow!" said the man next to me.

I nodded in agreement.

"Then," continued Jesus, "he put the man on his donkey and took him to the nearest inn, so that he could look after him."

"I've never met a Samaritan like that!" whispered the man next to me.

"Perhaps that's because we won't have anything to do with them," I hissed back, wondering if Jesus had finished his story.

"The next day, the Samaritan gave the innkeeper two silver coins and told him to look after the man until he was fully better. He promised to return with more money, should the innkeeper need it."

Everyone was silent and Jesus paused. Then he looked at the so-called expert. "Which of the people in this story was a good neighbour to the injured man?" Jesus asked.

The man shuffled uncomfortably. "The Samaritan," he said quietly.

"Yes," said Jesus. "So – be like the Samaritan!"

Chapter Four

There were times when the crowds left Jesus alone. Sometimes he insisted on it. He said he needed to pray, and to spend time with his Father God.

I didn't really understand it. I mean – I do pray whenever something awful happens, or when I'm worried, or when I go to the synagogue. But I'm never really sure what to do. It's difficult to find the right words to say. Especially when you're like me – just an ordinary sort of bloke, who's not very clever.

Anyway, one day Jesus had gone off to pray and the rest of us, his disciples, had gone with him. We just sort of hung around, not really sure what to do, waiting for Jesus to finish.

Suddenly I thought, this is really stupid! Why don't I ask him how to do it? He knows. He does it all the time!

So, as soon as Jesus had finished praying, I went straight up to him and said, "Can you teach us how to pray? I want to know."

Jesus smiled. "Yes," he said. "I'll teach you how to pray."

"How do we start?" I said, clapping my hands together in my enthusiasm.

"You begin by calling God 'Father'," said Jesus.

"Father?" John gasped.

"Father," repeated Jesus.

We looked at one another. We could hardly believe it. Jesus was telling us that we could call God our Father. All my life I had hardly dared call God anything at all, just in case I got it wrong, and now Jesus was telling me I could call God my Father!

"Then say," continued Jesus, "Father, your name is holy. May everything happen on earth as you want it to, just like it does in heaven. Give us bread to eat every day. Forgive us for all the wrong things we have done, and may we forgive others who have done wrong things to us. Help us not to want to do anything that is wrong."

I listened to Jesus' words and knew that I

would remember them. They were so simple. I'd always thought praying was complicated and you had to be clever to do it. But suddenly I realised that it was really very simple and anyone could do it. Anyone at all.

"Father," I said under my breath. "Your name is holy."

"If you ask God for something, he will give it to you," said Jesus. "If you look hard enough, you will find what you are looking for. If you knock at the door, it will open."

Jesus' words rang in my mind. He was so certain, so sure. Suddenly I felt a wave of doubt sweep over me. How do I know that God will answer my prayers? I thought. How can I be sure?

Jesus spoke. "Some of you are fathers," he said looking at us. We all smiled as we thought of our children. "If your son came up to you and said, 'Daddy, can I have a fish?' would you give him a snake instead?"

"No!" I said out loud. "Of course I wouldn't."

"Or if your son said, 'Daddy, can I have an egg?' how many of you would give him a scorpion?"

Nobody put their hand up. Well, you just wouldn't do it, would you?

"Of course none of you would!" said Jesus laughing. "You love your children, and you want to give them good things, even though you are only human and aren't perfect. Just think then. If you do this for your children, how much more will your Father God in heaven give good things to those who ask him?"

Chapter Five

One day, Jesus had been over to the other side of the lake, and when he came back, the usual crowds of people were waiting for him. I had never known such a crowd. He could hardly get off the boat.

I saw a man weaving in and out of the people. I recognised him straight away. It was Jairus, the leader of the synagogue.

The crowd let him through. Everyone knew Jairus.

As soon as he reached Jesus, he fell on the ground at Jesus' feet. I heard the people gasp and murmur in surprise.

"Look," whispered someone close to me. "Jairus is kneeling at Jesus' feet. Well..."

The voice faded away as I turned my attention to listen to what Jairus had to say. He was ringing his hands and his voice quivered with tears.

"Master!" he said. "Please come quickly.

My only daughter is dying. She's only twelve. Please come and help her. Please come!"

Jesus helped Jairus to his feet.

"I'll come," he said.

The crowd surged forwards. They'll crush him if they're not careful, I thought. I followed behind as Jesus slowly walked forwards through the crowd.

The walk was painfully slow. I could imagine how Jairus was feeling, and how much he wanted Jesus to hurry. But Jesus didn't rush. He just moved steadily forwards.

Suddenly he stopped, and the crowd drew back. "Who touched me?" he said. "Somebody touched me. Who was it?"

There was silence. Nobody moved. "Not me!" said someone.

"Me neither!" said someone else.

"Somebody did," said Jesus.

I looked about. Nobody was going to say anything. It was ridiculous. There were so many people that it could have been any-one. If someone didn't say something we'd be there all day.

"Jesus, everyone is pushing against you," I said. "It's impossible to say who it was."

"Somebody did," said Jesus, looking round at the faces in the crowd. "I know they did because I felt power leave me."

The crowd was still and silent apart from one small movement. Slowly a woman made her way towards Jesus. She was shaking and she knelt at his feet.

"I touched you," she said. "I have been ill for a long time. Twelve years. And I thought that if I could just touch you I

would get better. So I followed you in the crowd, and when I got close enough, I touched the edge of your cloak. Straight away I knew I was better. I felt well. I knew you had healed me." She hung her head and sighed.

Jesus bent down and looked at her. "You have been healed because you believed in me. Don't be afraid. Go in peace."

The woman stood up. She beamed at the crowd.

When will I learn to keep my mouth shut? I thought. Of course Jesus would know who'd touched him, he knows everything...

But my thoughts were suddenly interrupted as a man came barging through the crowd.

"It's too late!" he said, putting a hand on Jairus' shoulder. "Don't bother Jesus now. Your daughter is dead."

Jairus moaned and held his head in his hands. The crowd moaned and I moaned with them. Just when you saw something amazing happen before your very eyes, like that woman being healed, a disaster happened and Jairus' daughter was dead.

But Jesus' voice rung out. He put his arms around Jairus. "Don't be frightened," he said. "Just believe and your daughter will be well again."

I was shocked. Everyone was shocked. How could Jesus possibly say that this little girl would recover when he had just been told that she was dead? But then Jesus started to walk. His pace was quicker this time and he pushed Jairus on.

I struggled to keep up and the crowd gathered round us.

There was no doubt that the little girl was dead. You could hear the noise of crying long before we reached the house. The noise travelled round the crowd. Everyone was grieving for Jairus' daughter.

When he reached the house, Jesus turned round and faced the crowd.

"Stop crying!" he said. It was like an order. "Stop crying. The little girl isn't dead, she asleep!"

"Asleep!" I heard someone mutter as they tried not to cry. I knew what they were thinking because, if I'm honest, I think everyone was thinking the same thing too.

You're either dead or you're not! But there is a big difference between being dead and asleep.

"Asleep!" someone said with a sneer. "What's he talking about? This great teacher here thinks that Jairus' daughter isn't dead; she's having a nap!"

Then he laughed. And everyone laughed.

I felt awkward. I wanted to tell them all to shut up and not to laugh at Jesus! How could they, when they'd just spent hours hounding him, hanging on his every word. OK. So maybe he's got a bit out of his depth. Taken on more than he could chew. Maybe he should just have comforted Jairus and his wife – after all, we've all got to die sometime, haven't we? But at the same time I knew that if anyone could do something, Jesus could.

"Peter!" I heard Jesus say my name and I jumped. Did he know what I was thinking?

"Yes," I said, slightly sheepishly.

"Come into the house with me. And James and John, you come too."

We made our way through the crowd towards Jesus. I realised every eye was watching me. I tried to look confident, as though I knew what would happen next. But I didn't have a clue. None of us did.

The house was quiet and still compared to the noise of the rabble outside. The little girl's mother looked pale and her eyes were red and swollen. She didn't say anything but pointed to the bedding roll on which the lifeless body of the little girl lay.

Suddenly I wanted to cry too. She looked so frail and little. What could Jesus possibly do for her now?

Jesus crouched beside the bed. Gently he took hold of her hand and I watched as it hung limply in his. I hardly dared breathe. My heart was pounding.

The whole house was filled with a strange sensation, like the hot sultry air before a burst of lightning explodes across the sky.

"Little girl," whispered Jesus. "My child. Get up!"

What was he talking about? How could she get up? She was dead.

But I was wrong! Within a second the little girl shot to her feet. She was alive! She was completely well. She hadn't staggered or struggled or had to be helped up or had to be nursed. She had fully recovered!

Jairus and his wife rushed towards her and held her in their arms.

I looked at James and John and we reached out for each other too, clasping each other around the shoulders, unable to find the words to describe what we had just seen with our own eyes.

I looked at Jesus. He was smiling too. I wondered what he would do or say next. Nothing would ever surprise me again.

"Go and get her something to eat!" Jesus said to Jairus and his wife.

I laughed out loud. That was a surprise! I certainly hadn't expected him to say that!

Chapter Six

It had been another amazing day! Another amazing day in a long chain of amazing days, which had begun when I first met Jesus.

I'd just seen Jesus feed thousands and thousands of people with a little boy's picnic of five barley loaves and two small fish. With my own eyes I saw Jesus pass round the food and there was plenty for everyone. And there were twelve baskets of leftovers. I know that for a fact, because I helped pick up what was left!

What a day! But we were tired, and I could see Jesus was too. "Get in the boat and sail out across the lake," he said to a group of us who were his closest disciples. "I'll see to the crowd. I want to have some time by myself. I'm going up into the mountains to talk to God, to pray."

So we did as he asked, although I didn't

much feel like going out in the boat. I could see from the way the clouds were scudding across the sky that it was going to be hard work sailing over the lake, against the wind.

And I was right. We got to the middle of the lake, a long way from the shore, when the winds blew, circling the boat, buffeting us backwards and forwards and tossing us up and down on the water. The sails bulged and the ropes groaned. The sky grew dark and the waves tumbled and turned, crashing against the boat. We held on, trying to keep an even course, but making no headway against the strength of the wind.

"Hang on to the oars!" shouted James.

"I am hanging on!" I roared back.

"Row as hard as you can!"

"What do you think I'm doing!" I shouted, my voice drowned out by the howling of the wind.

"Look!" I heard Andrew shout.

"I can't look and row!" I yelled. "What do you want me to do?"

"Look!" screamed James and John in unison. They had let go of their oars and were standing, trying to keep their balance, pointing in the direction from which we had just come.

I turned to look, and immediately dropped my oar. Coming across the water was a figure. It disappeared for a moment against the blackness of the night as the clouds swept past the moon. Then the figure appeared again.

"What is it?" I yelled. "Who is it?"

"A ghost!"

With that a huge wave toppled the boat, sending us sliding and toppling towards each other, into each other's arms. We stood together and I was terrified. We all were. We stood and shook, holding each other, staring at the ghostly figure walking towards us across the water.

Suddenly I heard a voice: "Don't be afraid."

How many times had I heard that voice before? How many times had I heard that voice say, "Do not be afraid."?

I let go of Andrew and stared and stared.

I knew the voice. I knew who was walking across the water!

"Be brave!" said the ghostly figure, getting

nearer and nearer. "It's me: Jesus."

I heard the others cry out. But I wasn't afraid. I wanted to know. I wanted to know if this strange eerie figure walking towards me really was Jesus.

I staggered to the edge of the boat.

"Jesus, if it really is you, tell me to walk across the water to you."

I think the others said something to me, but I didn't listen. Instead I strained my ear to the wind, waiting for a reply. Then it came.

"Come and walk to me, Peter!"

It *was* Jesus! I knew it! I didn't hesitate. I lowered myself over the side of the boat. I put out one foot and then the other. But I kept my eyes on the face that I knew. It wasn't a ghost, it was Jesus!

I felt the weight of my body leave the boat, and I stood, my feet tickled by the lapping waves as if I was standing, paddling by the shore.

"I'm coming Jesus," I said, staring at him. I moved one foot and then the other. I was walking on the water! "I'm coming, master."

A great gust of wind blew me from behind and I lurched. What was I doing? How stupid and foolish I was! What had made me get out of the boat? Why did I think I could walk on water? Another gust of wind blew into my face and I screwed up my eyes as a sharp spray of water stung my face, and a wave slapped round my ankles. I was sinking!

"Help!" I screamed as a dark pit of panic opened up inside me and then exploded in my head. "Help!" my eyes looked around wildly at the furious clouds bullied by the wind and the roaring waves sucking me down into their icy inky depths. I couldn't see Jesus. Where was he? Perhaps it was a ghost, after all. "Help me!" I cried in desperation. "I'm going to drown!"

Immediately I felt a hand grab me. A big, strong, powerful hand, Jesus' hand. My feet grew steady once more on top of the water, and I clung to Jesus. "Why did you doubt?" said Jesus looking at me. "Have faith. Believe."

The panic had gone. I felt safe. We walked together towards the boat, across the water. Then we climbed aboard.

Straight away the wind stopped. Everything was calm and still, peaceful even.

I held tightly onto Jesus' hand and looked at the others in the boat. They were kneeling down, looking at Jesus. "You are special," they said. "You are God's Son, our Saviour."

Chapter Seven

Of course there was really only one question everyone was asking. It didn't matter who you were, whether you were one of Jesus' twelve special disciples, like me, or whether you were one of the crowd who followed him, listening to his teaching about God. It didn't matter whether you had seen some of the wonderful things he did, or whether you were a Pharisee who thought they knew more about God than anyone else. It didn't matter whether you were a Roman soldier upholding the Roman Empire. Everyone was asking the same question: "Who is Jesus?" Was he just a carpenter's son? Was he a troublemaker? Was he a prophet? Or was he really the special Saviour God had promised to send to rescue us?

Sometimes I felt absolutely sure who Jesus was. But at other times it all seemed so incredible that I didn't really know.

"Who do people say that I am?" said Jesus one day.

There were just the twelve of us there.

"John the Baptist!" said Philip.

"Elijah the prophet," said Nathaniel.

"Jeremiah the prophet," said Thomas.

"So what do *you* think?" said Jesus, looking around. There was an awkward silence. I mean, that was the big question, wasn't it? Who was Jesus?

Jesus waited. I thought back over the months I had spent with him. I remembered how Andrew had told me that he had met a man called Jesus and that he thought he was the Messiah, God's Son, his Saviour. I remembered all the things he had done: how he had healed people, and brought the dead back to life. And I thought about the things he had said: how he had taught us to live in a way that pleased God, how he spent time with God, and called him his Father.

In an instant my mind cleared. It was as if the sun had burnt away the morning mist, revealing a bright clear view. How could I question who Jesus was? I knew! I knew for certain! The words just tumbled out, as if they had power of their own.

"You're the Messiah," I said out loud. "You are the Son of the Living God."

Jesus stood up and looked at me. "Yes, Peter!" he said. "My Father in heaven has given you the answer to the question, who I am. God will bless you, Peter, and on you I will build my church."

A powerful shudder moved over me. But why was it that just when I'd found the answer to something there were still more questions? What did Jesus mean about building his church on me?

"Soon I have to go to Jerusalem," said Jesus.

"Why?" I asked.

"Because I have enemies. I have to go to the Pharisees and the Jewish chief priests. They will kill me. Three days later I will come back to life!"

"What!" I exploded. "That's ridiculous. You can't go up to Jerusalem when you know your enemies are there, and let yourself be killed. I won't let it happen!

It can't happen. I'll do everything in my power to..."

"Stop!" said Jesus.

I stopped. But I still couldn't believe what I was hearing. "You just see things as a human being," said Jesus. He was stern.

Of course I do! I thought. That's because I *am* a human being!

"But God knows better. He has other plans, and you cannot and must not stop them! Listen all of you," said Jesus. "You say you are my followers, but if you are really my disciples then you must not put yourselves first; you must follow me, even if following me is hard. I promise that if you do that you will not lose anything but will gain all the things that really matter, for ever and ever."

Just when I thought I understood, I still had more questions.

Chapter Eight

A few days later Jesus asked James, John and me to go up to the mountains with him. "Come with me," he said. "I want to pray." He often singled out the three of us to go to places with him. I wondered if the others minded. They never said anything.

We set off, climbing the hills, through the fields and the pasture, stopping occasionally for shade under the olive trees. We didn't say much. We didn't really know where we were going. Just spending time with Jesus away from the crowds was a treat enough.

Up we climbed, higher and higher. "How far are we going?" I whispered to James. He shrugged. "Don't know," he replied.

At last we reached the top of the mountain. I flung myself down on the ground and turned to look at the view. The whole world seemed to stretch before me.

"Wow!" I said. "It's beautiful, it's..."

I turned to look at Jesus. He looked different. I was rooted to the spot. Whatever was happening? What was happening to Jesus? I nudged John and he turned and stared at Jesus too. It wasn't my imagination, it was real! Jesus was changing before my very eyes. His face glowed and shone like the sun. It was so brilliant I could hardly look at him, but at the same time I couldn't turn away. He looked so beautiful. I watched as his clothes began to change as well. Gone were the grubby dusty tunic and cloak that he had worn as we clambered up the mountainside. Instead his clothes were a brilliant white, which glistened and sparkled like pure clean light.

"Jesus..." I gasped, trying to stand up.

But something else was happening. Two figures appeared, standing on either side of Jesus. They greeted him and spoke to him as if they knew him.

I watched transfixed. It was as if time stood still. I couldn't move.

"It's Moses and Elijah!" whispered John. "Moses and Elijah are here talking to Jesus." I could tell by the way he was talking that he was as awestruck as me.

Moses and Elijah! The very thought jerked me into action. Moses and Elijah had appeared on the mountain before my very eyes and were talking to my friend Jesus. This is wonderful! I thought. They must stay. They mustn't disappear. They must have time with Jesus.

I jumped to my feet and rushed towards Jesus. "Jesus, I've got a brilliant idea!" I said. "Let me build three shelters: one for you, one for Moses and one for Elijah..."

Suddenly we were surrounded by cloud and I lost my bearings. Where was I? What was happening? Then came a voice and my feet shot out from under me and I fell to the ground, quaking with fear.

"This is my Son," said the voice. "I love him very much and I am so pleased with him. Listen to him. Listen to him. Listen to him..." The voice echoed around me. It roared in my ears and rushed through my body as if it had touched every part of me, surrounding me and filling me. I screwed up my eyes and buried my face into the earth. My fingers dug into the ground, but my body trembled and shook.

I felt a hand on my shoulder and I cried out. This was it! I was going to be consumed by the voice. My heart thumped against the ground.

"Don't be afraid!" It was a different voice.

Slowly I moved my head and turned towards the voice, brushing the dirt from my eyes with the back of my hand.

It was Jesus. He was alone. Moses and Elijah had gone. He was back to normal. Then he bent over us and touched us. "Don't be afraid, James!" he said. "Don't be afraid, John! Don't be afraid." I listened to the words and the fear and the terror that had hammered my body faded away.

We walked down the mountain together. Before we got to the bottom Jesus said, "Don't tell anyone what you have just seen and heard. Not for the moment anyway. You can tell people what happened after I have been raised from the dead."

Don't worry, I thought. I won't tell. I couldn't begin to explain what I've just been through. They probably wouldn't believe me anyway.

Chapter Nine

From then on things started to change. For
a start Jesus kept talking about going up to
Jerusalem and dying. I didn't like it. I didn't
want to think about it. It made me feel
strange inside and very, very sad. And
things started to happen between us, his disciples. We began to fall out and argue with
one another. We wanted to know which
one of us was the greatest and stupid things
like that.

It wasn't just that, either. Things began to
change with the crowds that followed Jesus.
The chief priests and Pharisees were always
trying to trick Jesus into saying things that
would get him into trouble. I could see them
whispering and plotting. They didn't like
him, and I didn't like them either.

Oh, I know. I used to get fed up with the
crowds of people, and the jostling and the
pushing, but at the same time it was

wonderful. I knew I was right in the thick of something amazing: just watching Jesus heal hundreds of people was amazing, seeing the delight in the faces of the crowd as he told stories which at first seemed so ordinary – about sheep and shepherds, farmers and harvest. Suddenly realising that you weren't just listening to a normal story, but that you were beginning to understand more about God, and how much he loves you was incredible. Everything that had happened was terrific. And I suppose if I'm honest, I enjoyed being carried along by the excitement of being a friend of Jesus, who was so popular, and whom everyone loved.

But now things were getting nasty. Even I could tell not everyone loved Jesus. Some people hated him.

Nothing would stop Jesus. He was determined to go to Jerusalem. The twelve of us stayed with him. But I didn't like it at all.

We reached a little village called Bethphage. It was just on the outskirts of the city, on the Mount of Olives.

"Go into the village," said Jesus to two of

the disciples. "You'll find a donkey tied up there. Go and bring her to me."

"But what if..." I began.

"If anyone says anything, just tell them that I need it," said Jesus.

Honestly. I am sure Jesus can read my mind at times.

Before long, the two of them came back, with the donkey trotting along behind. We put our cloaks on the donkey's back and Jesus started to ride on down the road to Jerusalem.

I looked along the dusty road. There were a lot of people about. Perhaps they were going to market I thought, or...

But then I realised that the people weren't walking on; they were stopping alongside the dusty road, as if they were waiting for Jesus to walk by.

From every village along the road the people came. They brought their cloaks with them and threw them on the ground. They pulled branches off the trees and waved them in the air.

Wow! I thought. They're treating Jesus as if he were a hero who has just come back from winning a war. Anyone would think he was a king!

Then the crowd began to shout. "Hosanna!" they cried as Jesus walked past. "Hosanna to the king who is coming to save us!"

A wave of delight and relief rushed over me. Everything is going to be all right! I thought. Everyone loves Jesus!

"Listen to them!" I said to Judas. "Just listen to them."

"I am!" he said, rather shortly.

But I ignored Judas. "Hosanna!" I cried along with everyone else. "King Jesus!"

Everything's going to be all right, I thought.

Chapter Ten

But it wasn't really all right, even though I tried to kid myself it was. It's being in the city, I told myself. You're used to the country. You're missing the family and the fishing. But even though I knew there was some truth in that, it wasn't the whole story.

Things were getting serious. It was as if Jesus was looking for trouble. He kept challenging people, like the chief priests, who I knew were out to get him. Why can't he just leave them alone? I thought. But I didn't dare say anything.

Then, to make matters worse, Jesus went into the temple courts, where all the money changers and traders had their stalls, and he chucked them out. He overturned their tables, scattering money here, there and everywhere, and told them to get out. He said that they were turning his Father's house into a hideout for robbers, when it should be a place of prayer. Well, you can imagine what the priests and the pharisees thought. They were furious. They kept on at him, everywhere he went, asking him questions. "Who do you think you are to do or say these things?" they would ask over and over again. Jesus always had an answer. He called the chief priests liars! He actually called them snakes! He told people not to listen to them, not to do the things they said. It was asking for trouble.

And then he would talk to the twelve of us: long, long talks, in which he told us to watch out, to remember the things he had said about himself. I still didn't really understand what he was going on about. But I could tell it was important.

It was nearly time to celebrate the Passover Festival. Jerusalem was heaving. I wondered where we would go to have the Passover meal. But I needn't have worried. Jesus had made the arrangements. He had found an upstairs room for us to use. He just asked us to get everything ready.

Great, I thought. Just the twelve of us and

Jesus. It'll be great! A Passover to remember. I needed something to cheer me up, something to look forward to. I think we all did.

The table was laid with all the usual things: flat unleavened bread, a bowl full of bitter herbs, a roasted lamb and some cups for the wine. I stood back and looked. I had celebrated this festival once a year, all my life. Every year I remembered how God had rescued my ancestors from slavery in Egypt and had taken them to the Promised Land of Canaan. Every year. It always made me feel funny to think about it, but this year was different. Just being with Jesus and remembering the things that God had done made it different. More real, I suppose, because Jesus really did seem to understand all about God.

The twelve of us gathered round the table ready to eat. I looked at my friends, the other disciples. I could sense they all felt the same as me. This was going to be a very special Passover.

I glanced at Judas. He was standing away from everyone else, by the wall at the back of the room. He looked different. Shifty. Uncomfortable. But then he always did, or at least he had done for a while now. It was as though he wasn't quite one of us, didn't belong somehow. And he was always sidling off, disappearing on his own. I used to wonder where he went. Perhaps this meal would make him feel better, too.

There was a jar of water by the side of the room and a towel, ready for the servants to use, to wash the dirt off our feet. I pulled a face as I looked down at my own feet. They were caked in mud and dust. What a job! I thought. But that's city life for you.

Suddenly Jesus got up. To my complete surprise and horror, he wrapped the towel around his waist, poured some of the water into the bowl and started to wash Andrew's feet. Nobody moved. We were speechless. How could Jesus do something like that? I thought. It was outrageous. Jesus dried Andrew's feet and then began to wash Thomas's, then Matthew's, then James's.

And they just let him! I couldn't believe it! Washing feet was a revolting job. It was a job for the servants. Not for someone as special as Jesus. I wasn't just going to sit there and let him do that to me. It wasn't right, even though everyone else was just sitting there, like lemons.

"Are you going to wash my feet?" I said to Jesus. I could barely contain myself.

"Yes," said Jesus. He looked at me, and I knew he could read my thoughts. "You don't understand what I'm doing now, but you will do later."

"I'm not going to let you," I said. "I'm never going to let you wash my feet."

"Peter," said Jesus looking squarely at me. "If you don't let me you can't be my friend."

What had I said? Why couldn't I keep my mouth shut. Not be Jesus' friend? That was impossible.

"Then wash all of me!" The words spurted out. "Wash every single part of me!"

"There's no need," said Jesus. "Just let me wash your feet."

I did.

Chapter Eleven

The oil lamps filled the upper room with a warm, flickering light. We ate and we remembered all the things God had done for our ancestors.

"One of you will betray me," said Jesus.

His words cut through me. Betray Jesus? Never! Not one of us! Not one of his twelve special friends.

We stared desperately at each other. Who was going to betray him? Is it me? Is it me? It was an impossible thought and I felt a cold fear clutch me. Was it going to be me? Surely I would never, ever betray Jesus. I loved him. I had left everything to follow him.

"I won't be with you for much longer," said Jesus, "and this time you cannot come with me. Just remember to love one another. If you do this then everyone will know that you are my disciples."

"What do you mean?" I blurted out once again. My thoughts were wild this time. Not follow Jesus? Unthinkable. "Where are you going? I will follow you anywhere. I will do anything for you. I would even die for you!"

"Would you really die for me?" Jesus turned to look at me.

"Yes. Yes. YES!"

Jesus kept on looking into my eyes. He looked so sad. "Peter, before the morning comes you will have denied knowing me three times!"

"No I won't!" I said. "Even if everyone else disowns you, I never will!"

I knew I wouldn't. I was certain of it. How could Jesus say something like that?

We were all stunned. We had no idea what to make of it all. We just watched as Jesus picked up the bread and broke it into little pieces. "This bread is like my body," he said. "Take some of it and eat it."

We passed the bread round and ate. It stuck on my tongue. Why was Jesus talking in such riddles that made no sense?

He picked up the cup of wine.

"This wine is like my blood," he said. "It will be spilt, but it is a sign from God that he will make a new promise to forgive. Every time you eat bread and drink wine together, remember me."

I drank. I felt the wine swill round my mouth, and I thought of Jesus' blood. I felt scared. Something very big was about to happen. But I didn't know what.

"I am going to my Father in heaven, but I will not abandon you. Look out for me!"

It was then I noticed Judas was missing.

Chapter Twelve

We staggered out into the night. I was exhausted. But Jesus wanted to go to the Garden of Gethsemane to pray. After all I'd said I was going to stick by Jesus like tar. I wasn't going to be the one to let him down. And heaven help the person who does, I thought wearily.

We sank down onto the ground, resting in the gloom against the trunks of the olive trees.

"Peter, James and John," Jesus was speaking to me. I scrambled to my feet. "Come with me, while I pray," he said. "I am going to die and I feel so very sad. Keep company with me."

I didn't know what to say, I just followed Jesus deeper into the garden. I watched as he flung himself on the ground. He was clearly distraught. I had never seen him like that before. I felt sad and scared and sat watching.

"Wake up!" Jesus was standing over me. "Peter!" he said. "Wake up! Can't you stay awake with me for just one hour?"

"Of course I can!" I said wearily. How could I have fallen asleep at a moment like this? I must stay awake.

But a deep sense of exhaustion came over me. "I'll just close my eyes," I said to myself, "but I won't go to sleep!"

But I did. Jesus woke me again. I promised faithfully to stay awake. I really meant to. But I just couldn't help myself – sleep overwhelmed me.

"Are you still sleeping?"

I stumbled to my feet, rubbing my eyes. I felt sorry and ashamed. I had lost control. Nothing was as I thought. I hadn't wanted to go to sleep, but I couldn't help it.

"Come! We must go!" Jesus said. He seemed different, refreshed and revived, all fired up.

Suddenly there was a terrible noise and the garden was filled with flickering torches and rushing feet. There were men everywhere. I saw some of the chief priests' soldiers. They surrounded us. They were carrying swords and spears. I panicked and backed off. This was it! I was afraid.

I saw a man step out from the throng. He walked purposefully towards Jesus. It was Judas!

I watched in horror as the man who had been my friend walked up to Jesus and kissed him!

It must have been a signal, for suddenly there was this dreadful commotion. I felt round my waist and realised I had my sword. In an instant I pulled it from my belt and lashed out with it, slicing it downwards. I didn't care who or what I struck.

"Put your sword away!" ordered Jesus. I looked at him. I could save him, if he'd only let me. "Put it away!"

Slowly I put it in my belt. "There's no need for anyone to use swords. I'm not a troublemaker!" The mob went quiet. "You could have taken me any time you wanted, without the use of weapons. Don't you realise that all of this is part of God's plan and it has to happen? My Father God would send armies of angels to rescue me, if I asked him to. I am coming."

Jesus walked towards the mob and they seized him. I looked around. Where were the others? Were we just going to let them take Jesus away?

But the others had gone. They'd already fled.

Chapter Thirteen

I wasn't going to run away. I wasn't going to let Jesus down. No way! I was going to stick by him. So I followed, keeping to the shadows, making sure I stayed at a safe distance. I followed the crowds all the way to the high priest's house.

They were going to put Jesus on trial – there was no doubt about it. They were going to put Jesus on trial for breaking Jewish law.

I managed to get into the courtyard. Groups of the high priest's men were standing around the fires, talking and laughing. I hung around, trying to keep out of sight, but desperately wanting to hear anything at all about Jesus.

A servant girl was watching me. I pulled my cloak about my head and looked down. She stared at me. I could feel her eyes watching me, and I heard her feet walking towards me.

"You're one of Jesus' friends, aren't you?" she said. "You were with him!"

My heart missed a beat. "What are you talking about?" I said, looking defiantly at her. I could tell everyone was looking at me.

"I don't know anything about Jesus."

Another servant joined her. "This man was with Jesus in the garden!" she said.

"I promise you, I was not!" I said angrily. "I have never met Jesus in my life!"

"Well, you speak like one of his followers," said a man who had been sitting by one of the fires. I swung round to face him. "You come from Galilee. Anyone can tell that from the way you speak!" said the man sitting beside him. They got to their feet. Everyone was watching.

My heart was racing. I had to get out of there – fast.

"Listen!" I shrieked. "I've told you! I've never seen or heard of Jesus before. I don't know him, and I wouldn't want to either. I swear to you. I don't know Jesus!"

A chink of daylight glowed across the night sky. Somewhere in the distance I heard a cockerel crow in the morning.

I stumbled outside. And then I remembered. I had just denied knowing Jesus. My friend Jesus. The man I had promised to stay with for ever.

Tears flowed down my face. I wept and cried. Sobs of tears welled up inside me. I threw myself on the cold damp ground and moaned.

Chapter Fourteen

The next few days passed as though I was trapped in the grimmest and blackest of dreams. There was no escape.

Jesus had been arrested. They'd taken him away and found people who were prepared to tell lies about him. It made me sick. But I felt sick with myself, too. I was no different, was I? Lying was easy when you were up against it.

The high priest had handed Jesus over to the Romans. Pilate, the Roman governor had tried to get out of it. He didn't want a scene, but in the end he washed his hands of Jesus and sentenced him to be executed. Crucified.

The soldiers nailed Jesus to a cross at Golgotha and hung him up to die along with other criminals.

I had cried so much there were no more tears left in me. Why? What was the point?

What was the point of anything Jesus had done – healing the sick, telling people about God – if in the end he was just going to die like everyone else?

After a few hours of hanging on the cross, Jesus died. At least he wasn't in any more pain. The Sabbath was coming, and it would have been impossible to leave him dying over the Sabbath. So some of Jesus' followers arranged to have his body taken away and buried.

The rest of us – his disciples – stuck together. We were all so wretched and ashamed. We had all let him down, one by one. We had deserted him when he needed us most. We clung onto each other. There was no need for words. We all shared the same despair.

"Judas has killed himself," someone said. "He agreed to betray Jesus for thirty silver coins."

I couldn't pass comment. I'd betrayed Jesus, too.

But within my grief, I also realised I was scared. I was afraid of what was going to happen to me. Was I going to be hounded down and arrested? I felt sure that the chief priests would want to get rid of us all. Who would be next?

It felt as though we were waiting for something. But waiting for what? I tried to think of all the things I had heard Jesus say over the past three years, but my thoughts were jumbled. I remembered things, but at the same time the memories were overshadowed by this huge grief.

I lay awake, unable to sleep. The Sabbath was over. Now I could do something, only I still didn't know what. It was the first day of the week. A whole new day, a whole new week stretched before me. A day without Jesus. It was unbearable.

I knew that some of the women followers were hoping to go and give Jesus' body a proper burial, anoint him with spices and ointments, that sort of thing. Everything had happened so quickly, there had been no time to think or to plan. It was amazing that Joseph of Arimathea and Nicodemus had managed to organise a tomb for Jesus at all. But I suppose the authorities had wanted to get Jesus out of the way as quickly as possible. They wanted the whole business over and done with. "They've even posted guards outside his tomb," someone told us. Huh! I thought. They've got nothing to worry about now, have they? Why can't they leave Jesus alone? What harm can a dead body do?

Suddenly, through the darkness I heard the sound of running feet. My body stiffened. Was this what I had feared? Were these the guards that I so dreaded, coming to arrest me and take me away? Would I deny knowing Jesus again, just to save my neck? I lay still.

The footsteps stopped outside the house, and then the hammering began. "Peter!" shouted a voice. "Peter, come quickly!"

I threw off my covers and opened a shutter. There were no soldiers outside, only Mary Magdalene, a follower of Jesus.

"Let me in!" she said.

"Whatever's going on?" asked John, standing by my side, wrapping his cloak about him.

"It's Mary Magdalene," I said, unbolting the door.

Mary rushed in. She looked wild, as if she had been running.

"They've taken him!" she gasped, trying to regain her breath. "They've taken Jesus' body away!"

"What?" I exploded. "Why would they do such a thing? They've got what they wanted. He's dead. Now why can't they leave him alone?"

"I don't know." said Mary. "We went to the tomb early this morning. It was still dark. When we got there the stone had been rolled away and his body had gone!" She started to cry.

"Come on," I said to John.

We started to run through the quiet streets towards the garden where Jesus' tomb was.

John was quicker than me. He raced on. We zigzagged our way through the garden, until we saw it. The massive white stone which had sealed the entrance had been rolled away. John stood by the entrance. I could see he was looking in. "He's gone!" he said to me.

I pushed past John. I needed to see for myself. The inside of the tomb was cold and damp. The ledge where Jesus' body should have been was empty. All that was there were the strips of linen cloth that Joseph and Nicodemus must have wrapped around Jesus' body. They were in exactly the same place as they would have been if his body was there. I stared at them and a strange feeling flooded over me. Then I looked at the cloth that had been around Jesus' head. From the shape of it, his head might still be there. It was as if he had passed straight through it.

"Peter?" said John. He had come into the tomb and was standing by me. He too was staring at the strips of cloth.

"What do you think has happened?" he asked. "A grave robber would never have spent the time doing this, now would he?" he said, gesturing to the strips of cloth.

"No," I said and I shook my head. "What's going on?"

"Do you think..." began John. "Do you think that Jesus...?" He didn't finish his sentence.

"I don't know what to think," I said firmly. "Let's go back and tell the others."

Chapter Fifteen

"So, tell me again, what were the grave-clothes like?"

I took a deep breath and explained again. The nine faces of Jesus' disciples looked up at me. John sat by my side. I tried to be as patient as I could, but the tension was getting to me. We were all feeling the strain. We were all afraid. Everything had changed and become confusing.

There was a knock at the door. "Who could that be?" hissed Matthew.

"I don't know!" I snapped. "But there's only one way to find out." Cautiously I opened the door. It was Mary Magdalene.

She burst into the room and clapped her hands with delight. "I've seen Jesus!" she laughed. "He's not dead! He's alive!"

"What?"

Suddenly we were all on our feet. Mary couldn't keep still. She moved about us and flung her head back. "Jesus is alive. I've seen him!"

"Whatever do you mean? asked Andrew.

"Keep still for one moment, can't you?" I said. I couldn't keep up with all this. It made me feel anxious.

"I stayed in the garden, after you and John left," said Mary, staring straight at me. "I was crying. I felt so alone. Anyway, I went into the tomb, just to have another look, and there were these two men, dressed in white, sitting on the place where Jesus' body should have been. I was shocked. I couldn't move. But before I could say a thing, they asked me why I was crying. I told them I was crying because Jesus' body had gone, and I didn't know where it was. Then I knew that someone was standing behind me and I swung round. A man was standing there. 'Why are you crying?' he asked. 'Who are you looking for?' I thought he was the gardener. 'If you have taken Jesus' body away, please tell me where, and I will come and get him.' I couldn't stop crying. The tears just kept rolling down my cheeks. Then I heard someone say, 'Mary!'

I looked up and straight away I knew it wasn't the gardener after all. It was Jesus! I tried to touch him, but he said something about having to go back to his Father in heaven. And then he said I should come and tell you! Isn't it wonderful?"

Nobody said anything. We were too shocked to respond.

"Better lock the doors," I said after Mary had gone.

Chapter Sixteen

It was wonderful news. But it was also a bit scary. When Mary had gone and we'd bolted the doors and windows as securely as we could, we had to admit it. We were scared.

What does it mean? I kept asking myself over and over again. What's happening?

We stayed huddled together in the darkness of the room. Every now and then I glanced up to make sure the doors and windows were still locked. Every time I heard footsteps I was sure that this was it. We were about to be arrested, scooped up and identified as Jesus' friends, thrown into prison, tortured, and then...

But the footsteps disappeared and we were left comforting each other in the flickering light of a few oil lamps.

Suddenly I felt a movement in the air, like a gentle breath of wind. I looked up and jumped to my feet. There was a man. He was standing right in the middle of us.

"Who are you?" I whispered.

Everyone else was on their feet too. But as soon as I had asked the question I knew who it was. It was Jesus! Mary was right! He was alive.

"You're alive!"

"Jesus!"

"Master!"

"Teacher!"

The words just poured from all of us. Then he spoke. "Peace be with you."

It was as if, when he said the words, peace flooded over us. Everyone was quiet and still. Not only had we seen Jesus, but we had heard his voice too, and the words he spoke had such power, they made things happen.

"Look!" he said and showed us the palms of his hands.

Through each palm was a vivid red scar.

"Nails," I said. "That's the mark where they hammered in the nails, before they crucified you."

My thoughts swung back to that night, that terrible awful night, when nothing had happened as it should, when everything had gone wrong.

But had it gone wrong? Suddenly I wasn't so sure. Jesus wasn't dead, he was alive!

Before I could think any more, Jesus spoke again. "My Father has sent me, and now I am sending you. Receive the Holy Spirit."

Suddenly Jesus was not there any more. But somehow, I knew that he had not left us.

Chapter Seventeen

After that, we saw Jesus many times. He didn't stay for long, and we never really knew when we would see him again. But I always knew we would. Jesus was alive, but he wasn't around like he used to be. I sort of knew that something had to happen next. And, if I'm honest, I missed him. I missed being with him. There was so much I wanted to say to him, but I never really had the opportunity to do so.

"Come on," I said to Thomas, Nathaniel and a couple of the others one evening. "I'm going fishing."

"We'll come too," they said.

So we climbed aboard and set sail. But it was hopeless. We fished all night and did not catch a thing.

As the sun began to climb over the hills from the east we turned the boat round.

"Might as well go back," I said wearily.

"We're not going to catch anything now."

There was nobody about. It was too early. Then I saw a man standing on the shore. He raised his hands to his mouth and shouted, "Have you caught anything?"

"No!" I yelled back. If he thought he could get some fish from us, he was out of luck.

"Cast your nets on the right hand side of the boat and you'll catch some!" shouted the man.

What does he know? I thought. But maybe he could see the shadows and movements of fish in the water.

For some reason we all did as the man said. We picked up the empty net and flung it on the other side of the boat. Suddenly the boat jerked sideways. I knew that the net was full! I remembered another time, long, long ago when the same thing had happened. I looked at the man on the beach and I knew who it was. It was Jesus – and I had to go to him!

I threw off my cloak and leapt into the water. I swam and I waded. I ran through the shingle until I stood gasping and dripping alongside my friend Jesus. He smiled at me.

He had made a little fire on the beach and he was cooking some fish. There was some bread.

The others hauled their huge catch out from the boat onto the shore. The fish wriggled and slithered out of the net. There were hundreds of them.

"Bring some of them here," said Jesus to the others. "Let's have breakfast together."

We sat in friendly silence eating together.

If only we could stay like this for ever, I thought. Then everything would be all right.

At the end of the meal Jesus spoke to me.

"Come here, Simon Peter. I want to talk to you."

I followed Jesus. I wanted to have time with him alone. I wanted to tell him about that dreadful night in the Garden of Gethsemane, how I had let him down and told people that I didn't know him. I wanted to say how sorry I was. Sorry and ashamed.

"Peter," said Jesus looking at me. "Do you love me more than anything else?"

"Oh yes, Jesus!" I said. "You know that I love you."

"Then you must look after my lambs."

I nodded.

"Peter, do you really love me?" repeated Jesus.

"Yes!" I said. "I really love you."

"Take care of my sheep," said Jesus.

"Yes," I said. "I'll take care of them."

"Peter," said Jesus a third time. "Do you love me?"

I looked at Jesus. Didn't he know how much I loved him? Did he know that I would do anything for him?

"You know how much I love you, Jesus," I said. "I love you."

"Then Peter, you must feed my sheep," said Jesus.

Lambs and sheep! Whatever was Jesus talking about? Slowly I remembered some of the things he had taught us, when the crowds followed him, and we sat on the hillside together. He had said he was like a good shepherd and that his followers were like sheep.

My heart stood still! Jesus had told me to look after his sheep! He had given me a job to do. ME! Peter! The one who had let him down so badly, after all my brave bold words.

And I knew that Jesus had forgiven me. I knew that the past didn't matter any more, and although I didn't know what was going to happen next, I was sure that Jesus did.

Chapter Eighteen

Over the next few days we saw a lot of Jesus. We had no doubt that he was alive. He talked to us about God's kingdom and as if it was all terribly important. We ate meals together. "Wait in Jerusalem," he said one day. "Don't leave until you have received the special gift of the Holy Spirit which my Father in heaven has promised to give you."

We listened. But we still didn't understand. "When the Holy Spirit comes," said Jesus, "you will also receive the Spirit's power. Then you will be able to tell everyone in the whole world about me!"

Suddenly a cloud came down. I tried to see Jesus through the cloud, but he had gone, vanished within it, as if he had gone up into the sky.

It had happened so quickly and without warning, just like it had on that other occasion, when a cloud had come down and God had spoken.

"Why are you looking up there?" said a voice from behind me. I jumped. We all did. There were two men, dressed in white. I felt sure that they were angels.

"Jesus has gone to heaven!" they said. "One day he will return to earth in the same way that you have seen him go!"

After that we went back to Jerusalem, and waited.

When I say "we" there were quite a few of us – not just the eleven of us who had been with Jesus all the way through, but other believers and followers, some women, Jesus' mother and his brothers. There were about one hundred and twenty of us altogether. We just wanted to be together, to talk about him, to remember to do the things he said, like praying to God. We did a lot of praying together.

It was strange, but after my talk with Jesus on the beach, I felt different. I could see people looking at me, asking me what I thought. At times, I felt as though they were looking to me to lead them. It was a bit scary really, because I didn't know anything much, only what I had seen and heard Jesus do and say. I'm only a fisherman, I kept saying to myself. "What sort of a fisherman?" said a little voice inside. "A different sort of fisherman? The sort that catches men and women for God?" It was just a thought.

We waited and waited in Jerusalem, staying in houses, meeting together as often as we could. It wasn't easy. At times I felt like a caged animal, waiting and waiting. But I knew that we had to wait. So we did.

Jerusalem was getting busy again. It was fifty days after Passover, the time for the next festival celebration in the Jewish calendar. There were loads of visitors and travellers from all over the world. But we stuck together and waited.

On the day of Pentecost itself we had all arranged to meet. More prayer. More chat.

I heard a strange sound. It sounded like there was a violent storm brewing and a wind blowing. Suddenly, I felt the wind rushing through the house. It swelled and it tore through us and around us. We blew and shook in the wind, like the sail on a boat, swollen into life by the swell of the wind. Before we had a chance to speak, the house was filled with little tongues of fire. They danced and flickered about the house, touching us, warming us, until each of us had a tongue or flame over his or her head.

This is it! I thought. This is what we have been waiting for! This is the Holy Spirit!

I heard a tremendous noise, like a crowd of people. I looked about my friends and realised everyone was speaking, and I was speaking too. But I wasn't speaking Aramaic, I was speaking another language. My mind and my tongue had a life of their own.

We all looked at each other in amazement and started to move out of the house, onto the street.

By this time a crowd had gathered outside. They must have heard the noise. I could tell by looking at the crowd that there were people from all over the place. "How can these men speak all these different languages?" I heard one man say.

"They're only simple Galileans."

"They're talking about God," said someone who looked as though he had come from Egypt. "I can understand every word they're saying."

"I come from Crete," said someone else. "They're speaking my language. What's happening? What does it mean?"

"What does it mean?" echoed the voices in the crowd.

"I'll tell you what it means!" piped up a voice. "It means that they're drunk! They've had too much wine!"

Suddenly I felt a huge surge of power explode within me. I knew what I had to do, but at the same time I knew that I wasn't doing it alone. Jesus was with me. God's Holy Spirit was in me.

I held up my hand and stepped forwards. Everyone was quiet.

"Let me tell you what is happening!" I said in a loud, clear voice. "We're not drunk. It's only nine o'clock in the morning! Long ago God promised to send his Holy Spirit, and this is what he has done today. Let me tell you about a man called Jesus..."

The words flew from my mouth as I told the people everything I knew about Jesus: how he had been God's Saviour, how he had lived and how he had died, how he had risen from the dead and returned to his Father in heaven.

"Everyone here should know that this is true," I said loudly and clearly. I could hardly believe it was my voice! My thoughts were so clear. I knew exactly what I had to say. Never in all my life had I imagined I would be able to speak to so many people. "Jesus is God's Son, our Saviour, the Messiah. And you wanted him crucified."

I could tell everyone was listening. The whole crowd was quiet and still. But then a babble broke out as the people whispered amongst themselves.

"But what can we do about it?" shouted a voice from the crowd.

"Yes," cried someone else. "What can we do? It's too late for us to do anything about it."

"What shall we do?"

I looked behind to my friends. They looked at me smiling, encouraging me to go on. I turned to face the crowd. They were immediately silent.

"Repent!" I said. "Say sorry to God for all the wrong things you have done, and be baptised in the name of Jesus. Then God will forgive you and he will give you the gift of his Holy Spirit just as he has done for me."

The crowd began to break up. Some shuffled away, into the narrow streets of Jerusalem, in small groups, twos or threes. But others stayed. Hundreds and thousands of others stayed.

"Baptise us!" they cried. "Help us!"

We set to. There were so many people, but I knew that each one was important, each one needed to hear about Jesus. Suddenly our little group had grown in numbers and in strength – all in one day, and I thought back to all the things that Jesus had told me, how he had asked me to look after his lambs and to feed his sheep.

Fishing. Four years ago I never thought I would do anything other than fishing. But then I'd met Jesus, and he taught me how to be a different sort of fisherman. The sort that tells men and women about God.

I wondered what tomorrow would bring. I wondered where God would ask me to go or what he'd ask me to do. But I knew that everything was going to be all right. Jesus was with me. God had given me the gift of his Holy Spirit.

If you've enjoyed this book, why not look out for...

"Looks can be misleading, can't they? I mean, you can look at a person and think how cool and calm they are. But that's not always right, is it? Take me, for instance. I know that I look strong and tough. I look like a leader, which is just as well really, because that's what I am. But inside it can be different, scary even."

Joshua tells us what it was really like to change the Israelites – a bunch of grumblers – into a lean, mean fighting machine, ready to invade the Promised Land. And how God gave him the strength he needed.

ISBN 1 85999 451 2

Available from your local Christian bookshop

"I didn't feel nervous because I knew that I was doing what the Lord God wanted and he was the one who was really in control. 'This is it!' I shouted. My voice boomed across the mountain. 'People of Israel, from today you will have to decide who you are going to worship – God or Baal. We'll ask both of them to send down fire from heaven and the true God is the one who sends down fire!'"

Elijah tells us what it was like to be one of God's prophets when Queen Jezebel was determined to kill him. At times he was running for his life. But whenever Elijah felt very alone, God had already got a plan in place.

ISBN 1 85999 452 0

Available from your local Christian bookshop

"I can't stand my brother! Do you know what I mean?

It's a shame really, because we're twins. But we're not identical. No way! I haven't got anything much in common with him. He's big and hairy. And I'm, well, smaller - just about right. Yuk! Esau's gross! He's so big and hairy. And he fancies himself."

Jacob tells us his story. He may have started out as a bit of a wimp but he changed inside with God's help. He even wrestled with God - and lived!

ISBN 1 85999 444 X

Available from your local Christian bookshop